HIGH NIGER

AND

DELTA OF THE

NIGER

ISBN: 9781695836433

©

HIGH NIGER

AND

DELTA OF THE

NIGER

JUAN SANZ SANZ

CLARIFICATION:

In 1983, after years of thorough studies, many calculations and verifications, JUAN SANZ SANZ (1943 - 2019), announced, privately and personally, and in two different instances that then seemed the most suitable for evaluation and the possible implementation of the ideas it provided, the following proposals: IDEAS FOR A PROJECT FOR THE USE OF THE HIGH NIGER WATERS IN THE IRRIGATION OF THE ALUVIAL PLAINS SITUATED TO THE WEST OF TOMBUCTU and CULTIVATION OF THE DELTA OF THE NIGER.

Unfortunately, the very cultured man has just passed away, a self-taught man who many would not hesitate to describe as a prototype of a person close to the Renaissance, given the large amount of knowledge that he sought to enlarge throughout his existence.

The baggage that provided his wisdom, due to the depth of the immersion he did for decades in Geography and History, together with the careful observation of how much was happening in those years throughout the Planet, it was for the author the necessary momentum.

It is good to remember again that we speak of 1983, so, as in the present 21st century, the word weighed heavily against him, always present in a hierarchical in excess: SELF-TAUGHT.

Without moving a comma from his legacy, JUAN SANZ SANZ's work is published for the first time under the title he chose: HIGH NIGER AND DELTA OF THE NIGER.

BIOGRAPHY:

Self-taught, Juan Sanz Sanz (1943-2019), devoted himself, from early youth, to unravelling the problems posed by the readings of historical events narrated by the various authors who frequently diverged from each other.

Geography was one of his great hobbies and reason for fervent study, not existing on the planet place, no matter how remote it was, that had not been fully informed.

The attentive follow-up of the social and political reality in which its existence took place resulted in proposals for water use on three continents and each of the projects was sent in its day to the places that were most suitable for its achievement.

Languages - French, English, Italian, Portuguese and German, in addition to his own, Spanish - had no secrets for him and thus he could fully enjoy the Literature written in them, another hobby in which, As an enlightened man, he found his peers.

In early youth the Spanish guitar and later the piano, were musical instruments to which he dedicated a great effort similar to the passion that the music awoke in him and thus, in maturity, with authentic devotion and delicacy, he interpreted beautiful pieces of Bach , Chopin, Debussy and Beethoven who contributed a lot to make their days more human and the passage of time milder.

In addition to the Water Projects, it leaves many literary works practically about to be edited, something that will be made public.

In memoriam

INTRODUCTION

NIGER RIVER:

Born at 1,800 msm, 250 km from Konakry and Freetown. It runs peacefully towards the NE, to Timbuktu for 1,200 km in a straight line. In recent geological times it ended here, the two joined sections form one of the longest currents on Earth, 4,200 km, the same as the Yellow, for example. About 200 km before reaching Bamako enters the plain; Here the difference in width between flood and runoff is 600 meters. An arch of rivers carries the waters of a 500 km mountain front, where the rains are extraordinary (much more than 2 m.) Before arriving at Bamako, it stops receiving constant tributaries; The parallel course of the Bani benefits from a territory with seasonal rains and temporary water courses. Below Bamako, it crosses a flat plateau and the swamps and parallel arms begin. A vast swampy region of 60,000 km2, the Macina, which ends in Timbuktu, extends on both sides of the main course to a distance of more than 100 km. The width of this region is more than 200 km and its length are more than 400 km.

An underground stream follows from Timbuktu an ancient bed of the Niger to the North. The wells of the Aruan oasis, 260 km from Timbuktu, show, albeit posteriori, the ups and downs of the Niger level. At the height of Timbuktu, the swampy region ends; in river it is directed towards E and then to SE. A little below Gao the floods begin, which do not end until Yeba; in a section of more than 1,000 km the river is not navigable. From Niamey the summer rains are abundant. The summer flood of its high course reaches the Curve in New Year and the lower course in March or April.

The rains of the lower course produce a flood in September. That is why the lower Niger has two floods: one in April and one in September, while the high one only has one at the end of summer. In Bamako, the flow rate is 10,000 m3 in September, but in waste it is reduced to 20 or 30. Together with Yeba, this flow has become 8,600 in flood and 280 in waste. Further down comes Benue, with a constant high flow. Niger floods do not provide fertilizer slime. The flood progresses very slowly because the course of the river is very wide and has to fill the banks first kilometres and kilometres away.

For three months, from mid-August to mid-November, the Niger has been carrying a flow in excess of 5,000 m3 / s in Kulikoro (next to Bamako, capital of Mali). Precisely in

Kulikoro begins a stretch of flows that reaches the vicinity of Sansanding. It is at this point where the vast interior delta begins, which covers a huge surface beyond Timbuktu. The extension that annually covers the waters is enormous. The amount of water lost by evaporation in this region, called Macina, is several thousand cubic meters per second. So the river leaves the swampy region with an extremely depleted flow. The large volume of water that it carries at the mouth comes from the coastal countries of Guinea.

The idea is to correct this natural phenomenon. For millennia,

Niger has flowed into this inland lake similar to Tchad, but even larger, since the volume of water in Niger-Bani is greater than that of Chari-Logone. Thus, during millions of years the floods have been filling this plain, until it becomes practically horizontal. One of the keys to this matter is that the drainage of this swamp region It is extremely difficult due to the lack of unevenness. If the main riverbed was lowered, perhaps the waters could be exited. But the problem is that these waters do not need to be expelled but should be used higher. The general idea is to use the waters of the Niger outside the swampy region.

The current Niger has a tendency to go north, to lose itself in the Sahara; It is the trend of the Nile and Chari. If the data provided by the subsoil plan that we have at hand are true, it gives the impression that for long ages the river was pouring northward and that only when the coastal Niger caught it, from Gao, it began to pour towards the East, carrying out a work of reduction of the valley in this sense, leaving the alluvial regions of the North, which today are a desert steppe. If this desert steppe formed by floods really exists - we don't have to doubt what the books tell us - there is a dry alluvial region, surely fertile, that could be used with the simple slope of the river, since it is practically the same level than this one.

The first thing we have to do is make sure that this alluvial region is as stated in the manuals. If so, the project is extremely simple and feasible. Simply divert the river through a region without slopes, in the direction of North and Northwest. It is about distributing the water during the flood season, taking advantage of it instead of letting it be lost by evaporation and sterilizing a region as extensive as the one it covers today. This would also prevent the flooding of the Macina, which for the most part would be dry after a few years. The river would run exclusively through a riverbed and if the Macina was still partly flooding it would be due to the flooding of the Bani, its main tributary, which flows into this region regardless of Niger. More precise data are needed on the river regime, on what would be the really usable flow in the event that its waters were retained in the stretch of flows between Kulikoro and Sansanding.

The most convenient thing would be to build a large reservoir in the region of the streams, which retains the waters of the river and allows an exhaustive use of its waters. If the large flood of the Nile is 7,500 m3 in September and its average flow of just under 2,000 m3, we can assume that the Niger regime is similar to that of the Nile.

Let us not forget that this alluvial region was the center one thousand years ago of the Empire of Ghana, whose existence was based on the use by wells of a water table almost flush with the ground that has subsequently been exhausted. It has, therefore, this alluvial region located to the NW of the river something special. If the waters of the Niger were diverted and distributed through canals, the result would be a very important agricultural nucleus, capable of feeding a good part of the inhabitants of this part of the

Sahelian strip, plagued by chronic hunger. It would be a medium-term solution.

CHAPTERS:

ONE

Today, almost all Third World countries have a notable food deficit. Food production growth evolves more slowly than population growth. This food deficit is accentuated by the general demand for a better standard of living. All this rests on the lack of agricultural resources and it is, in short, the crisis of world agriculture that, in reality, we have to face. If Third World countries had developed agriculture, the overpopulation phenomenon would not be noticeable.

So, we have to ask ourselves: why is the agriculture that sustains most of the world's population unable to provide enough food, when in those countries there are, apparently, the basic elements for it: land, rain, temperate climate? It is a paradoxical phenomenon that we must explain.

The current agriculture crisis is simply that it is not capable of producing what is necessary in every place where it is needed. Food products should not be subject to excessive exchange; when society conducts a large trade in agricultural products, it is a sign that we are facing an anomalous situation. These, due to their low price and large volume, must be produced in places of consumption or a short distance from them. Only in exceptional cases the phenomenon has a positive character, it is not a tare; for example, the Great Britain of the last century or the Venice of other centuries, industrial centres of enormous profitability that could afford not to produce most of the food they consumed. But, generally, when the phenomenon that we are attending in our time appears, that the consumer centres do not produce the food they need to survive, it is a sign that we are immersed in a state of things of a negative nature. In a healthy economy, exchanges of agricultural products should be reduced to what is strictly necessary. As is known, this is one of the principles on which the European Economic Community rests. Trade must deal with products of higher price and lower volume: manufactures, on the one hand, mining and agricultural goods, on the other, whose production is located in certain places and, therefore, is necessarily lacking in others. Basic subsistence products - not just foodstuffs - must be obtained at the consumption centres themselves, reducing their exchange to a minimum. These are elementary facts, well known, which is worth remembering.

In recent years, there has been a growing increase in the exchange of agricultural products, the result of insufficient production in many countries, in contrast to the superabundance of others. This situation needs to be corrected, because countries whose production is insufficient, can hardly be supplied in the world market of agricultural materials. Indeed, although the productions of the countries that export basic foodstuffs are of high profitability and, therefore, of moderate prices for their own production system, these prices are far from the purchasing power of the deficit countries. There are foods in the world, perhaps in sufficient quantity, but they cannot be the object of a commercial distribution that meets the general needs.

This is the situation in which we now find ourselves. The plague of hunger is spreading very slowly across the planet and, little by little, formerly self-sufficient countries or food surpluses go on to swell the ranks of the poor. It is a strange, anomalous situation, and proves the principle set forth above that food products must be produced in consumption centres.

TWO

So, what is the reason why agriculture in Third World countries is not able to meet their food needs? Until a few decades ago this production was sufficient, except in times of drought or major catastrophes. However, in the case of China, for example, food shortages were the cause of social upheavals that began in the middle of the last century (*). But, the problem is the low productivity, the low performance of Third World countries, located in tropical areas almost entirely.

While, in the northern countries, the North, agriculture has been subjected to intensive use, the yields of tropical agriculture are very low. In the South there are potential agricultural resources in an amount greater than the North, but these resources are exploited only in a minimal part. The current means of exploitation in the South have reached the limit of their possibilities and a radical transformation is necessary.

In the South there is greater extension of working lands, the warm climate allows to obtain crops without interruption. However, despite these favourable conditions in theory, their yields are low and the extent of land used occupies a proportional part much lower than the North. There are larger areas of cultivated land in the North today. However, the food capacity of tropical lands is much higher than that of the boreal.

The agriculture of the North is a reflex agriculture of the industrial centres to which, first, it supplies. In it, the elements of industrial activity have been projected on the modes of production. And, thus, the mechanical, chemical industries, the transport, treatment, conservation, and research devices, act directly, obtaining very high yields, although the fertility of the boreal countries is inferior to that of the tropical ones.

For natural agriculture, with minimal intervention from modern industry, two conditions are necessary: fertility and humidity. These two conditions occur to a greater extent in tropical countries, despite their vast desert extensions, than in the North. However, the agriculture of the South does not happen to be a natural agriculture, in which the lack of a powerful industrial activity prevents that it is transformed in the same way that the agriculture of the temperate countries has been transformed.

That is to say, the agriculture of the countries of the North is only the reflection of their industrial level, while the agriculture of the South is also the reflection of their industrial vigor. Hence, the solution of the problem has been tried frequently from this principle. It is necessary to put things in place. It has been tried to raise the industrial level of the South so that it is reflected on agricultural production, transforming it.

(*) *This document was written by the author in 1983.*

THREE

The agriculture of the South must transform itself, be the principle of economic development. For this it is necessary to bring into play the favourable factors that it is endowed and obtain from them the best possible performance. Naturally, everything costs money; but those investments that are destined to the fantastic end of promoting an industrialization, if they were dedicated to another more accessible and positive purpose, would undoubtedly promote a really definitive transformation.

On the other hand, tropical agriculture has reached the limit of its possibilities. He cannot give more of himself with the means he currently has. New elements must be introduced. The basic transformation that the countries of the South must carry out consists in the application of irrigation in an exhaustive way. Irrigation multiplies agricultural production and corrects climatic irregularities.

It is necessary, if you want to solve this problem, to take full advantage of the resources available to these countries. What are these resources?

The great extension of working lands, the abundance of rains, the good weather. Until now, these conditions have been used in an elementary way, with limited participation of man, which partially corrects Nature, but does not dominate and transform it.

Tropical agriculture does not progress and is not able to provide the food that is necessary because it is not transformed and this transformation cannot come from the application of an industrial technology that does not exist there, but from the modification of its productive bases. Until now, these have been the soil, the rain, the animal fertilizer or through burning and, to a lesser extent, irrigation. Only in the overpopulated Asian countries irrigation has developed, but in a rudimentary way, generally without the application of modern technology. The productive base of tropical agriculture should be the use for this purpose of the hydraulic resources - water and energy - of tropical rivers. Systematizing this principle is the only formula to solve the tremendous problem of an agriculture that has reached the limit of what it is capable of producing by its own means. The project that we expose next, around the use of the Upper Niger, It is an example of how the implementation of this principle can achieve exceptional results. This is the only way to, in the short term, solve the frightening problem of the food deficit; in the medium term, to establish the bases for a firm and autonomous economic development; and, in the long term, to bring these masses, which total more than 2/3 of the world's population, into the modern life of which, as a whole, they remain on the side-lines.

FOUR

In the Sahel countries the oscillations of the periods of drought and humidity are the consequences of the notable variations of the precipitations that occur from one year to another. When it rains little, the weather dries and the desert move south. This is the cause of the desert strip moving forward or backward, depending on the rains being, together, greater or lesser. And all this in a capricious and irregular way, without really knowing the cause and discovering the rule.

To these irregular oscillations in the mass of rains that fall on the Sahelian strip correspond advances and setbacks of the desert. In the wet years, the vegetation advances towards the North, the crops are obtained with great ease and abundance. In the years with little rainfall, desertification is accentuated and extends more and more. This is the situation suffered by the Sahel for several years (*). The desert advances towards the South, the arable strip narrows, the rain crops give a diminishing yield and in many regions they are impossible. Food capacity is reduced in such a way that a situation of extreme hunger occurs.

It is clear that these countries cannot continue to depend on the rains to get the food they need. It takes another way to produce them. This can only be the use of the waters of the great rivers of the region. These are born in territories of different climatic conditions, with less pronounced oscillations; They are a relatively constant pluvial power supply, which ensure a minimum flow.

Niger and Senegal collect waters from territories where it always rains in abundance, despite drought cycles. This is the factor that can counteract the variable factor that is the Sahelian climate.

(*) This document was written by the author in 1983.

FIVE

As is known, the High Niger or Yoliba is born in the Fouta Djallon massif, a region near the Atlantic coast, where it rains extremely, and pours into the interior of the African continent. It collects the waters of a long mountainous front, little elevated, near the coast, which does not form a screen to the summer winds loaded with moisture, as happens, for example, in the Himalayas. It rains abundantly on both sides of this low mountain range.

The waters pour towards the Northeast, towards that great plain that is the Western Sahara.

Until a geologically recent time the Upper Niger and the Lower Niger were two different rivers, the first flowing, like the current Chari, into a large lake at the edge of the desert, while the second was born in the Adrar and followed the lower course from the current Niger; its head is in the Oued Tilemsi. Thus, this independent river that was the Upper Niger was going to be lost in a large lake, of which the rosary of lake swamps that border its course, far from it, between Segou and Timbuktu are remains. The ancient lake, similar to the present-day Chad, stretched across the rugged region and extended westward from the river in the direction of the Hodh.

Upon the capture of the Upper Niger by the Lower, the waters of the old lake had an exit and only some swamps remain in the region near the river. But the bottom of the flooding region, located to the west, emptied, remaining a vast alluvial plain. This is the area, outside the floods, that could be exploited. If it really is the bottom of an old lake and was covered by river floods, we are facing a territory of agricultural land that is easy to use.

It is not necessary to carry out any previous drying and conditioning operation. It is enough to divert water from the river to it, in contrast to the region of the banks of the Niger, covered with swamps and subjected to large floods, increased by the fact that the river, to leave it, narrows in the area of conjunction with the lower Niger. The riverine region today forms a vast inland delta, with very little slope, covered with lakes. Its drying is very difficult. On the other hand, next to this swampy plain there is another dry one, which has the same origin and is the one that should be used.

For this, it is enough to divert the waters of the river to a sufficient height so that the canal dominates the whole of the dry alluvial plain. As the slope is very small, it is necessary to collect the waters in the highest part of the plain, in its beginning by the West. That is, in the Bamako region. Here the river leaves the bottom of hard beds and enters the floodplain. Between Bamako and Koulikoro the river passes a region of streams, which disrupt navigation. This is the point that should be the origin of a water diversion channel. It is 340 meters above sea level and seems sufficient to dominate most of the northern plain. However, the Niger is bordered in this part by a strip of low hills, which the canal will have to cross to exit to the plain. This is, in short, the idea. It is about taking advantage of the fertile land at the bottom of the former lake of Niger, now out of the flood, having changed the structure of the river. And all this through a simple deviation.

During a long geological period, the Upper Niger landed in this interior region, with no access to the sea. Throughout that time there have been numerous climatic alternations; relatively dry and other times of high humidity. The African continent is very old; its orographic distribution has changed little. The main work that Nature has subsequently carried out has been the erosion of the ancient mountains and the clogging of the intermediate basins. That is why the continent has that typical form of interior basins, filled with alluviums, surrounded by very worn ancient mountains. The process of formation of the alluvial plain that interests us is nothing more than one of these mechanisms of erosion and clogging. In this case, the Niger course has been the main instrument, although we must not forget the wind flooding; the wind called harmattan, dry desert wind, blows constantly for more than half of the year, in these regions. That is to say, the combined action of the Niger alluvium and the dust transported from the desert by the harmattan has resulted in the filling of this inner basin, surrounded by ancient massifs except for the North, where there are extensive territories of fixed dunes In the center of the Sahara the dunes are quick, but in the limits of the Sahel they are held by the vegetation.

SIX

The drying of the Macina and the whole of the swampy and lake regions that the river covers with the summer avenues could be attempted, lowering its level in the lower course. But it is a stretch of river of many hundreds of kilometres, with very little slope, practically horizontal. Although the river level was lowered, there are large areas that would not be drained. On the other hand, the great avenues, of 12,000 m3 / second of maximum average, would be a constant danger for this low region.

The desiccation of the swamps is an extremely difficult task, while the diversion of the river towards that other portion of the former alluvial plain of Niger is relatively simple; It only requires a bypass channel. It would be necessary to cause a reduction of the bottom of the bed of the Niger of many meters between Timbuktu and Gao for this aquatic plain to empty spontaneously. Even so, it would be necessary to enclose the river between dikes so that the great flood would pass by. If there was no choice, this is what should be done. On the other hand, the former alluvial plain of the Niger, formed when the river had no exit to the coast, is extended to the west by a dry region, outside the floods. This is the factor that we can take advantage of immediately, without the need for colossal works or impractical investments.

The work of building an artificial channel for 1,000 kilometres in Niger from the swamps is incomparably more expensive than simply diverting to the floodplain to the west. Even so, the Bani River would continue to flood the current swampy region, maintaining a large part of the swamps, unless this river was enclosed between hundreds of kilometres of dikes.

It must be taken into account that the Bani river flows into this plain and must be regulated. At a later stage, after the regularization of this river, its waters could serve to form a second colonization front, now in the swampy region. The idea is to allocate the waters of the Yoliba to the dry alluvial plain, while those of the Bani to those of the swamp. This river is also born in the rainy strip of the Guinean coast, but it crosses regions less rich in rainfall than the Niger and its flow is lower. Despite this, in the medium term, the Bani could carry out this colonizing work.

Another possibility is to divert the Bani to Niger at the height of Bamako. These rivers run parallel to hundreds of kilometres, a short distance from each other. The course of Bani seems to follow a slightly higher height. If the Bani has its channel at a higher altitude than the Niger at the height of Bamako, the diversion of its waters to that seems a relatively simple operation.

The regularization of the river system would immediately produce a consequence: the desiccation of the Macina and the rest of the swampy region to Timbuktu, as the lake water is not renewed through annual flooding. If these floods of 12,000 m3 on average, do not flood the plain, it would cease to be a swamp in a few years. With this, the territory near the great river would be open to colonization, either by the expansion of the irrigation device, or by rain crops. The dry alluvial plain has no dense vegetation, requiring complicated deforestation. It is covered with shrubs and grasslands and its cultivation should not present excessive difficulties.

SEVEN

The diversion of the Niger through the hills would be enough to cultivate a strip of land whose extent will be determined by the flow of water that the river can provide constantly. The average river flow will be approximately between 1,500 and 2,000 m3 / second. This means, at 20 km2 / m3, an extension of between 30,000 and 40,000 km2, that is, between 3 and 4 million hectares. With this distribution of water, 15,000 m3 / hectares are provided per year, enough to obtain more than one crop.

If we calculate that alluvial lands under intensive exploitation, with two crops per year, can feed more than 1,000 people per km / 2, the capacity of the enclave would approach 50 million inhabitants, which is as much as the population of surrounding countries (*). If, on the contrary, the whole of the floodplain is used, by means of a single annual harvest, the result will be the same, but the cost of putting it into operation, much higher. So it is necessary to choose the alluvial lands that most easily lend themselves to their cultivation.

A channel that collects the waters of the Koulikoro (where a regulation reservoir that reaches Bamako itself) must be installed, must cross the region of hills that separate the river from the northern plain.

The colonization phases could be the following:

One. Use of the water flow of its flood, through diversion, through a channel: a harvest. From mid-August to mid-November the flow of the river remains above 5,000 m3 / second.

Two. Regulation of the head of the basin, retaining the water of the whole of the year: Two crops. A large reservoir in Kourousa and other minors capable of retaining the volume of water and supplying electricity for a beginning of industrialization.

Three. Collection of the waters of the Guinean rivers, diverting them to the slope of the Niger. Extension of the cultivated strip.

Maybe you could make better use of this extraordinary rain spot that is the massif of

Fouta Djallon, capturing some rivers that are born on the opposite side. The massif is very little abrupt. Niger's water flow would increase in that way.

The first phase is relatively easy to perform. It only requires the construction of a diversion channel. The second already needs large investments in dams but would allow the establishment of power plants.

This second phase could be carried out gradually, on the wealth generated by the first.

The alluvial region has been created by the river, where it has been flowing for a long geological period. The means available to me do not allow me to reach a precise knowledge of their characteristics, which cannot be different from those of other similar basins. We can only know exactly the general fact, which seems sufficient. According to the geological plane that is at hand, this region extends in the form of an irregular triangle that has as vertices Bamako, Timbuktu and the Hodh. The extent of this floodplain land can be calculated at 150,000 km2. About half are formed by the swampy plains on the banks of the Niger. The other half will correspond to the region outside the floods, located to the west. The usable territory of be more than 50,000 km2. If it were possible to irrigate them completely with the waters of the Niger, an oasis comparable to that of Egypt would emerge in the middle of the desert, capable of feeding a population no less numerous than that of that country; The plague of hunger in Western Sahel would be overcome. As the population of the surrounding countries is far from this figure, a good part of the crops could be dedicated to the production of agricultural raw materials, which would be the origin of industrial activity. This will be a firm development principle for those regions. Not only would the tremendous problem of the food deficit be overcome, but the basis for constant economic progress would be established. The electrical stations of the regulation reservoirs will supply a good part of the necessary energy. The cultivated enclave of Upper Niger would be the driving force that set that part of the world in motion.

We have with it an example of the principle set out above that the development of the economy of tropical countries must begin with the use of river resources: water and energy. It is the only basis on which its support in the future will be possible.

But this is not the only transcendent consequence that would derive from the project, as we will see later.

(*) *This document was written by the author in 1983.*

EIGHT

The dry alluvial territory that lies to the Northwest of the Niger Arch was the center of the Ghana Empire, which, as is known, has nothing to do with the current state named so. From the beginning of the Era a powerful commercial center was developed in the limits of the desert, that maintained a constant traffic between the Mediterranean and the Sudan. This trade was based on the export of gold from the alluvial sites of Bambuk, in one of the tributaries of Upper Senegal. This forested region was not dominated by Ghana, which was limited to transport to the Mediterranean ports through the desert. Another essential element of that trade was the salt of the salt marshes of Idjil, of which the Sudanese peoples were in great need. Arab travellers have left us a description of that amazing civilization. But the support of the State was the cultivated fields that, in the middle of the steppe, were irrigated with the waters of the shallow wells of which the region had an overabundance.

Later the water table dropped, making agriculture impracticable. In the centres of Kumbi Saleh and Audoghast, rich angels provided travellers, at a great distance from Niger, with the equipment and provisions for crossing the fearsome desert obstacle. At the present time an arm of the Niger leaves from Sansanding towards the North through the steppe and formerly it extended towards the Northwest, feeding the subalveal layers of the region in which Ghana had its origin. On the other hand, an underground channel of the Niger still runs through the oasis of Aruan, whose wells show up and down the river level at a distance of 200 kilometres.

The region thus has an interesting historical tradition; It was the center of what has surely been the most developed and vigorous society of how many have appeared in the Sudanese strip. For centuries Bambuk's gold was the only source of supply for that metal. Its high value made trade through the desert profitable. Recall that during the final period of the Roman Empire gold is imposed as the main traffic currency and this phenomenon is accentuated during the Byzantine era and the beginning of the Arab; Thus, gold coins disappear almost entirely from Western Europe during the Byzantine era, absorbed by Mediterranean transactions. The main supplying center for the golden metal was the Sudanese river deposits. But this traffic would not have been possible without the existence of a point of support in the middle of the desert region, which by special circumstances provided the means of subsistence with which to make the crossing the large empty space.

NINE

And it is precisely the restoration of a nucleus cultivated in that region that may allow us to resurrect the ancient routes and bring the Mediterranean countries back into communication with the Sudanese, the North and the South. If the colonization of the territory were possible in the simple way that we propose, we would have the advanced point on the desert from which to attempt its transit.

It is not the least of the causes that maintain the backwardness of the South the fact of being separated from the industrial countries of the North by a wide desert strip that hinders and limits exchanges. This strip isolates the North of the South, prevents direct coexistence and relationships, in fact, can only be done by non-terrestrial means. From Senegal to Manchuria, a wide desert line dampens commercial and, above all, human relations. The South and the North are brutally separated by hundreds of kilometres of dry, semi-empty lands, with few intermediate support points, through them, relations, if they exist, are carried out extremely precariously.

In the New World, we cannot ignore the importance that the deserts of North Mexico and the Southwest of the United States mean for traffic and relations. Air and sea traffic, with all its importance, do not cease to have a secondary value from the point of view of the coexistence of societies. Only terrestrial communications can promote contiguity, close coexistence. In our time, through this strip there are only a few open routes, at a great distance from each other, which are at all points insufficient to promote the intimacy that is necessary between the North and the South.

Where the phenomenon occurs most extreme is in the Sahara, which radically separates Europe from Tropical Africa. There is no commercial route that can meet the needs of intense communications between two continental masses that are, at the same time, the extremes of the North-South polarity: the center of maximum irradiation and that of least receptivity. The cause is none other than those 2,000 kilometres of empty spaces. Recently some strategic roads have been built (*), at the cost of enormous efforts, but this purpose is not enough and perhaps with the irrigation of the floodplains near the Niger we had the base to solve the problem.

(*) *This document was written by the author in 1983.*

TEN

Among the obstacles that hinder trade relations and migration, the most serious are the desert territories. These can be of several types: arid spaces, swampy regions, large forests. The jungles have frequently limited the activity of man, as well as the extensive swamps. But the obstacle to par excellence for circulation has always been the desert, where the lack of water and food has made travel into true odyssey. That is why man has not given in to him; He has not hesitated to try the adventure, stimulated by the benefits he could obtain from his transit, caused by the company's own difficulty.

On the African continent we find the biggest obstacle. They are the 2,000 kilometres of Saharan strip, with few intermediate support points, that grows or narrows according to the season or the climatic cycle; with its sandy beaches and immense spaces covered with pebbles. In a space almost as vast as the European continent, all its dispersed springs provide travellers with a volume of water of a few tens of cubic meters per second, those that run along a small European river. The rare and torrential rains, over the millennia, have created groundwater layers at varying depths, which appear capriciously according to the nature of the terrain. The flow of water that the desert treasures is very scarce and is renewed with extraordinary slowness. If it is exploited in excess, the water table drops rapidly; Over the centuries it has only declined, and the water is obtained in greater depth.

This phenomenon explains why, having not changed the climate since the last glaciation, water is becoming increasingly scarce and must be obtained at greater depths. Travelers find that the desert is increasingly arid and opposes major difficulties in its crossing.

For maritime navigation, the desert strip was also an insurmountable barrier until the introduction of modern sailing, which allowed us to move away from coasts where it was impossible to supply water. The radius of action of the Mediterranean paddle galleys was determined by the time when the water remains potable. This time is very short and that is why the navigation was for "Finis terrae" for thousands of years to the Hesperides and Cape Bojador.

Perhaps the trip was made on occasion, exceptionally, but a regular navigation system between the Mediterranean and the coast of

Guinea was never established. On the other flank of this strip, the Red Sea suffered from the same overhead. The Egyptians had to develop a system of terrestrial communications, tracing the Nile and crossing the Ethiopian mountains to the monsoon influence region, whose mechanism they discovered in the Hellenistic era. This land route made the fortune of Axum and Meroé, precisely because along the Red Sea the old ships could not maintain a regular trade.

The first commercial trips by land that we have news of are the "car routes", which linked the Mediterranean ports with the Sudan.

At that time the water table was still high, and the circulation of cars and horses was possible. At the beginning of the Era the dromedary is introduced, capable of performing much longer stages and faster. Thanks to this, the springs, which used to be mere points of support on some trade routes, are subject to agricultural exploitation, becoming oases or angels. Its extension and demand for water has only grown, lowering the level of groundwater and forcing them to look for them in distant springs, whose flow is transported to the main oasis through underground channels, the foggaras. The modern machinist, which rescues water hundreds and thousands of meters deep, is ending not only with the reserves of filtered water in recent times, but with fossil waters, from rains that occurred thousands of years ago.

The desert is increasingly deserted; Water is scarcely increasing. The chasm that separates Europe from Tropical Africa widens, despite attempts to save it with some strategic communication channels. All this has no other cause than the depletion of water resources. Since the desert cannot give itself more water, it is necessary, to solve the problem, to introduce water from the surrounding countries. It is in that sense that the High Niger project would acquire unusual significance.

ELEVEN

It would be enough to derive a small part of the Niger water flow from the plains of the Hodh so that it would be possible to establish a Trans Saharan route. An aqueduct that originally had, for example, 50 m3 / second, would serve as the basis for direct communication between Europe and Tropical Africa. This water flow, which represents only 1/30 or 1/40 part of the flow

Niger, it is as much as the one supplied by the Sahara spring complex. With an almost exact orientation from South to North, it would cross the desert precisely where it is narrowest: between the last foothills of the Atlas, facing the Canary Islands, and the Niger Arc region. We saw above that it was the advanced position on the desert of the angels of ancient Ghana that allowed a regular communications system to be established over a thousand years ago.

Now that device could be restored, in a much more solid and lasting way, by running through the desert an aqueduct that would supply water and food with the land transit. A line of oasis, from stretch to stretch, would link the Maghreb and the Sahel. Along this populated line it would be possible for a highway to run easily, since the water would isolate it from the desert; in reality, it would not cross the desert, but a succession of oases a short distance from each other. The desert is not as barren as it seems; it is enough that a light shower humidifies any point so that it fructifies splendidly, since the lack of rains maintains its richness in fertilizing minerals. Western Sahara is a low and flat plain and through it the aqueduct would find few orographic obstacles. Probably, the water runs by simple gravity from the Niger to the mouth of the Draa, because in its origin it will have a altitude above 300 meters above the sea.

On the basis of this great water pipeline, a communications system that meets the needs of our time could be established: highway, rail, oil and gas pipelines. In recent decades road transport has evolved considerably, gaining in speed and load capacity. This is how long-distance transport systems have been established in other parts of the world. The device that we propose here between the Mediterranean coast and that of the Gulf of Guinea, would be of similar dimensions to the one that exists in North America, from Coast to Coast. The first base of its profitability would be the products obtained in the Upper Niger irrigation, which are very far from the sea; there is almost the same distance to Dakar as to the Atlas. The hydrocarbons of the Guinean Coast could follow the same path to Europe.

Only the terrestrial communications manage to provoke a true coexistence between the towns. Tropical Africa today has the structure of a large island; their transport to the outside world is done by sea or by air. For a radical transformation to take place, it must be connected by land to the industrial North. Its structure must be modified, cutting it from island to peninsula; Its isthmus could be the proposed communications line, based on the regulation of the Upper Niger.

During the colonial era, France was the hegemonic power in this part of the World and tried to establish a line of communications that had these milestones: Paris, Marseille, Algiers, Arch of the Niger, which proved impracticable; trade continued to pour into the coastal ports.

They were other times and road transport had not evolved. Now it is possible to install a land route, fast transport, capable of absorbing and distributing Euro-African trade.

Starting from the Strait of Gibraltar - where it would be

inevitable, later, to build a bridge -, it would reach the Arch of the Niger and then the Gulf of Biafra (these are the three major strategic points of the area), branching as it approaches the Niger, precisely in the region that we propose to colonize. Between the Strait of Gibraltar and the Hodh the line would be unique; but in the region of new crops of the Upper Niger it would branch in all directions, towards the Guinean coast: Dakar, Konakry, Fretown, Abidjan, Accra, Lagos, Douala, and towards Central Africa: North Nigeria and Lake Tchad.

Thus, the new cultivated enclave would be the axis of an extensive long-distance land communications device. A part of the infrastructure is carried out: the railway lines and the roads that connect the Sudanese strip with the Guinean ports: Dakar-Bamako, Konakry-Kankan, Abidjan-Uagadugu, Lagos-Kano. The device terminals are established, and the work will only have to be completed, unifying it and giving it a direct exit to the North. That is, the current communications system, oriented towards the South, would change direction, heading towards the North and grouping into a single device.

The water of Niger will make possible the culmination of the old Trans Saharan dream and a new era will begin for Africa. Thus the exceptional utility of the risks of the Upper Niger will be twofold: not only will it solve the problem of the food deficit in the Sahelian countries, but it will also be the basis of a Euro-African communications system, making it possible with its waters and becoming on its axis.

Author's page on Amazon:

Amazon.com/author/juansanzsanz

www.ingramcontent.com/pod-product-compliance
Lightning Source LLC
Chambersburg PA
CBHW061712250726
48657CB00002B/601